TERROIR

Also by Robert Morgan

TERROIR

ROBERT MORGAN

PENGUIN POETS

PENGUIN BOOKS
Published by the Penguin Group
Penguin Group (USA) Inc., 375 Hudson Street, New York, New York 10014, U.S.A.
Penguin Group (Canada), 90 Eglinton Avenue East, Suite 700, Toronto, Ontario,
Canada M4P 2Y3 (a division of Pearson Penguin Canada Inc.)
Penguin Books Ltd, 80 Strand, London WC2R 0RL, England
Penguin Ireland, 25 St Stephen's Green, Dublin 2, Ireland
(a division of Penguin Books Ltd)
Penguin Group (Australia), 250 Camberwell Road, Camberwell, Victoria 3124,
Australia (a division of Pearson Australia Group Pty Ltd)
Penguin Books India Pvt Ltd, 11 Community Centre, Panchsheel Park,
New Delhi - 110 017, India
Penguin Group (NZ), 67 Apollo Drive, Rosedale, Auckland 0632, New Zealand
(a division of Pearson New Zealand Ltd)
Penguin Books (South Africa) (Pty) Ltd, 24 Sturdee Avenue, Rosebank, Johannesburg
2196, South Africa

Penguin Books Ltd, Registered Offices:
80 Strand, London WC2R 0RL, England

First published in Penguin Books 2011

LIBRARY OF CONGRESS CATALOGING-IN-PUBLICATION DATA
Morgan, Robert, 1944–
Terroir / Robert Morgan.
p. cm.—(Penguin poets)
ISBN 978-0-14-312019-3 (pbk.)
I. Title.
PS3563.O87147T47   2011
811'.54—dc22   2011025826

Set in Bembo Std
Designed by Ginger Legato

147204767

To the memory of my mother
Fannie L. Morgan, 1912–2010

CONTENTS

TWO

ACKNOWLEDGMENTS

Grateful acknowledgment is made to the editors of the following publications in which many of these poems first appeared:

Antietam Review, Appalachian Heritage, Asheville Poetry Review, The Atlantic, Bat City Review, Crossroads, Fresh, Jabberwock Review, The New Blue Ridge Cookbook, North Carolina Literary Review, Now & Then, Oracle, Rivendell, River City, Shenandoah, Smartish Pace, Southern Poetry Review, Southern Quarterly, Southern Review, and *Tar River Poetry.*

"Cow Pissing" first appeared in *The Generation of 2000,* Ontario Review Press, 1984.

"In Memory of William Matthews" first appeared in *Blues for Bill,* University of Akron Press, 2005.

Several of these poems were included in the chapbook *October Crossing* from Broadstone Books. Special thanks to Larry Moore and Jonathan Greene. Some were first published in a special issue of *Southern Quarterly,* Spring 2010, edited by Jesse Graves. Thanks to Jesse Graves, Michael Mcfee, and Robert West for their editorial wisdom.

TERROIR

IN MEMORY OF WILLIAM MATTHEWS

A veteran insomniac,
if you had ever slept, you could not
have read so much and thought so much
and written so many pages.
Even awake, the rest of us
were never as awake as you.
I was in awe of your alertness
and your articulateness. I've
never met another who talked
so long and well. Tradition meant
a lot to you. You were a connoisseur
of wines, of things Italian, of
custom shoes, who would forget
to match or even to wear socks.
Of our generation you were the most
generous behind the mask of irony.
What is there to say now you are dead?
You were both old before your time
and younger than the rest of us.
That meant a lot to me, that
and your enthusiasm for words
and your quick snarls about the nature
of nature poetry. Bill,
wherever you are now, I'm sure
you're laughing at the way we poets
take ourselves so seriously.
And I concede the fault, except

I want to say I took you seriously
and was not wrong. Your death keeps on
astounding me with jolts of sadness,
as I think I'll never hear your voice
again or get a letter filled
with needled gossip. The book is now
both closed and open, the last
dinner and last jazz savored
in the fine hours over brandy
and smoke that hung like incense in
a Hindu temple everywhere
you lived. I want to note that you
were loved and that your work is loved
and will be. That's the final flower
I bring to lay at the place of
memory, even as I hear you snicker
beyond the wall of silence: Send
no flowers, bub, but maybe some
good claret might not be unwelcome.

ONE

OCTOBER CROSSING

The woolly bears go cross the road,
their backs of orange and black a sign
of winter's length and strength to come.
They inch across the lanes in fur
fit for a monarch, fox, or star,
as crows descend and yellow leaves
fly out against the twilight breeze.
However accurate the widths
of colors on their prophet backs,
or knowledge of their fate as moths,
they seem intent on crossing this
hard Styx or Jordan to the ditch,
oblivious to the tires' high pitch.

The biggest trees in woods will fall
and knock down lesser trees and lie
out level on the slope beneath
a gap that spoils the canopy.
The trunk then rots inside its hull
of bark and floats in leaves for half
a century, a fallen god,
a relic of fertility.
The carcass hollowed out will spill
rich compost from its shell and house
a bear or host a fox or skunk.
But as the giant molders down,
and seeds take root in mineraled rot,
new sprouts appear along its length
and soon a line of saplings claim
the breast of the old corpse that bears,
like Johnny Appleseed's canoe,
a trove of seedlings in the wild
to land them on the future's shore.

TERROIR

That quality that seems unique,
as thriving from a special spot
of soil, air flow and light specific,
and also frost and winter sleep,
conditions of particular year,
as every instance comes just once
with mix of mineral and grease,
what Hopkins chose to call inscape,
or individuation, sounds
so close to terror you'd confuse
the two, as if the finest and
the rarest blend would come with just
a hint of fear or pain, the sting
and shiver of revulsion with
the savor of the earth and sun,
of this once, not returning, sung
for this one ear, on this one tongue.

BACKGROUND RADIATION

Here at sunset the prehensile tendrils
of the pole beans are translucent as twists
of optical fiber. Last rays flood the horizon
and pull away into the outer dark.
The glow beyond the hills suggests background
radiation that astronomers have measured
at the farthest reach of instruments,
intrinsic luminosity and rumors of
creation's first flash rushing away
at ever greater speeds, as though all matter
repelled itself at the end in reverse
gravity, like something almost perceived,
almost remembered. For everything is
thinning out, is rarefied and getting
distant on a logarithmic scale. In
the beginning was light that gave birth to
dark energy and fluctuations in
the very fabric of space-time recessing
and decaying. But once the sun is gone, all
the other stars wink on, wink on, and show
the strange and far topology of night,
geometry of sky and darker ridge.
A cricket carols in the grass, and the river
shivers its bright rubble, ripples out
its trigonometry and balance quick

as the simple addition and subtraction
of human time and sight, to which we cling
like pole beans to the lattice of the strings.

COW PISSING

First the tail begins to stiffen
at its root. The thick base rears and
a warp runs out the length of the
appendage to the dirty hank
and the whole is lifted slightly
to the side, exposing the gray
puckered pussy. But it's how the
back arches up that startles, how
she humps as though bracing against
and backing into something hard,
pressing to release a valve or
tip a cask open. And the stream
that starts comes as though from a hose
not round but flattened by her lips.
Shot on the pasture dirt, the jet
wears out a basin that overflows
into tracks and sprays gold mist on
hooves and grass, shivering rainbows.
When the blast lessens and scalds down
to tatters and drips and is done,
she whips the tail a few times to
knock off the last drops and walks on
to graze. The puddle glistens like
gold wine in the sun, and crackles
as it soaks into the splash track.
The grass sparkles many colors
where the growth will be less for the
libation a while, and then more.

DEW

It's something of a mystery,
this minute rain downloading from
the sky so slowly and invisibly
you don't know when it came except
at dusk the grass is suddenly wet,
a visitation from the air,
precipitant from spirit world
of whitest incarnation or
reverse transfiguration, herald
of river, swamp and ocean breath
sent heavenward, released to earth
again to water weed and stone,
and shatter rainbows in the sun,
the purest liquid that exists,
too fine to slake our human thirst.

The best spot may not be a mountaintop
or tower, for there you're deafened by the wind
that's fippled by the gap or ridgeline.
An open field is better, giving space
for listening's pause. But better yet go down
into a dip or gully floor where air
is calm, and hear the whisper, hush, and soothe
of shining mist above made audible,
articulate in stillness far below,
as stars are said to speak at noon
to those in well or dungeon.

The deer beside the highway, dead
and bloated so its legs shoot out
like barrels of some obscene bagpipe,
seems ready to explode, as flies
revolve and fizz around the eyes
and mouth. The stench downwind is black
and suffocating. Yet a few
days later you walk past the thing
in summer heat and find it's been
deflated: only rags of hide
and gristle, hair, and bits of bone
are scattered round, now greased with rot
and sinking out of sight in flood
of rising weeds and goldenrod,
each atom of corrupted flesh
identified and sorted, hauled
away by scavenging coyotes,
by maggots, worms, bacteria,
each bite sent to its proper place
to feed the needy multitude.

SOFT MOUNTAINS

Unlike the Rocky range or sharp
Sierras or Cascades or Alps,
the Appalachian peaks are called
soft mountains in comparison.
Their rounded tops and smoothed-out slopes,
now cushioned by leaf-rot and mold,
betray their ancient age, worn down
to knobs and nubs and fuzzy balds
of brush and trees and laurel hells.
But underneath the thicket swirls
and fallen leaves and stingy soil
they're granite at the core and hard
as any hill in Cappadocia,
the softness only in the face,
deceptive to the look as steel
encased in velvet, hardness at
the heart, while flanks are petal-smooth
and quaint and blue as old-time music.

IN TERROR

In winters when deep snow was sealed
with glaze of freezing rain, the deer
with pointed hooves punched through the shield,
and trapped up to their bellies in
the thickest drifts, their legs were held
so firmly they could neither step
nor leap, their heat just melting crust
to set again and lock them cold
in terror. They remained till dusk,
when wolves appeared with brightest moon
that paved the field with platinum
as though it were Elysium.

FERN GLADE

As wind stirs through an opening in woods,
green feathers long as plumes on peacocks write
in pools of sunlight from the canopy.
And what they scribble must be dank as earth
with ink of roots and alphabet of worms
and rot of last year's leaves and fallen bugs.
The syllables they seem to scratch now rise—
yes, levitate—a spinning hologram
of vapor glittering in the shaft of light:
a visitation of illuminated gnats
above the shadowy glade's scriptorium.

SEISMOGRAPH

The tiny pen on slender arm
records the tremors and the lulls,
so sensitive to planet's stir
it writes an endless picture
of rest and jolt and magnifies
the shivers we don't recognize,
the deep frisson, the mantle twitch,
and then goes wild with crazy swings
to represent vast demolitions
of mountains toppling in ravines,
and buildings crashing into dust,
to bury thousands in rubble,
all written down in coolest ink,
a diary, polar, manic.

PEEPERS

The choral outcry by the pond
one final winter afternoon
sounds less like little peeping chicks
than scream of some far-off alarm,
as though a locked door had been sprung.
But what do peepers glimpse from pool
and marshy bank and weed and brush
or willow branch? Do they foresee
the coming weeks of fertility
and rampant mating in the mud
and eggs laid by the myriad?
Or do they look ahead to drought
and winter cold and warn themselves
and all who hear of gulping fish
and salamander, preying bird
and foraging squirrel, the certain end
of summer's procreative binge,
foretelling frozen pond and grave?
Or do they simply celebrate
the moment, seize the day they have
with melancholy song of love,
as humankind are known to do?

INSPIRED

The mouths of giant caves are known
to breathe in during winter months,
then slowly start to sigh out air
as spring slows into summer heat,
as if the earth itself inhaled
and exhaled once a year in turn
and kept the rhythm but for bats
that swoop outside at twilight, then
return at dawn to roost as drops
of fur. The threshold sings with warm
air whispering toward the summer sky,
then hums as wind that's chilled and shrunk
falls back across the cavern's lip.
The throat between the worlds is thrilled
with constant music of the shift,
no matter how the planet tilts.

CONVOCATION

The little sulfur butterflies
go bouncing over weeds and hay
fields stretching to the edge of woods,
suggesting conflagrations at
the heart of air and dancing sparks
that wrestle in the breeze with dust
and clearest Brownian molecules.
The wind's a frenzy in this show,
a carnival that rhymes in small
maneuvers with the larger fall
and swing and rise of planet, star,
of galaxy and far quasar.

BOND

Two trees, so similar and close
in age they might be twins or mates
or even married, rub against
each other every time a rain
or wind disturbs the forest calm
and makes them veer and lean and neck
to chafe a spot on flesh that's raw
and tender, hurt so long and deep
they cannot heal. In quiet they stand
with dignity apart, upright
in sylvan company until
another gust excites and stirs
the canopy. They groan and cry
out from the gall of closeness, touch
and moan and bawl and bark and can't
escape the wound of intimacy.

TRANSLATION

Where trees grow thick and tall
in the untroubled wild,
the older ones are not
allowed to fall but break
and lean into the arms
of neighbors, shedding bark
and limbs and bleaching silver
and gradually sinking piece
by piece into the bank
of rotting leaves and logs,
to be absorbed by next
of kin and feed the roots
of soaring youth, to fade
invisibly into
the shady floor in their
translation to the future.

POISON OAK

Does anybody understand
how poison oak just seems to know
to plant itself beside a tree
or fence post? What intelligence
enables such a trailing shrub
to choose a place where it can climb,
as if the seed could see what host
could lift it into prominence?
The instinct in the germ to find
a partner for its destiny's
exact: how the vine will cross
a meadow just to claim a spot
at base of oak or hickory
and draw a thread of poison out
of earth. The climber sews itself
to bark in stages, stitching up
into the light for maximum
exposure, guided sure as by
an intuition to make contact
with summer heat and passing skin,
its pretty leaves in trinities
for spreading its smart medicine.

DESCENT

The boulder at the mountain's foot
always resembled a fat whale
with lichens on its curling lip
and moss as thick as barnacles
across its scaly back. It was
a mystery how the rock got there
in woods without another stone
in sight. I wondered if the giant
had washed there in some ancient flood,
been stranded far from river's verve.
The mammoth pebble grinned and grinned
its crevice smile as though it had
a secret, beached and left so far
from origin in water's rage.
But when the trees were bare in fall,
I glanced at cliffs revealed way on
the mountain's peak above and saw
the lineage and the true descent
of kinship with the mountaintop
from which the boulder rolled and stopped.

PROPHET

The weathered trunk of bristlecone
that twists in ancient whirlwind torque
on highest ridge of continent
and leans in the prevailing roar
is reaching for the distant plains,
a relic of momentous war,
persisting since the glacier.
Now it's outlived all things that grow
upon the planet. See, it holds
out like a torch of sparkling green
the needles on one withered arm
to pass on to the next eon,
a word still spoken from the root
of knotty elder burning heart,
the history that is also prophet.

ORACLE

The spring high on a mountainside
goes murmuring from the lips of rock,
and what it whispers seems to tell
of endless wandering and return
across the pathless wilderness.
The moss is luminescent on
the logs, in spotlights from the trees
that search the pools and foamy leaps
as water swells against a stone
and ripples under stress until
it spills a silver tongue on air
and drops into the next reserve
with syllable of prophecy
that sounds more like an elegy.

HILL WIND

A hill wind will surprise you first,
for air on hills is slanted up
or down. It tends to climb a slope
or sink along a mountainside
into the darker hollows. In hills
you find no level breeze but cold
wind draining from a summit line
or hot air rushing upward from
the valley floor on summer days.
Or wind will curl around a hill,
compressing and rebounding as
it wrestles with a barrier to
its passing, turbulent against
obstruction, boiling over, fights
itself and bites its tail in wild
frustration. Air on hills cannot
be still, but fidgets, stirs, and whispers,
aspiring on to greater heights
to freedom of the infinite,
or plunges back to darker depths
in search of cooler, promised rest.

THE BIG ONE

The thistle from a frost-dead weed
flings out across the winter field,
a dry fly flourishing on the breeze.
But no fin leaps into the light
to snag the luminous trick of sight
that catches only our attention,
until it catches earth, the big one.

SNOWSPOUT

The blizzard wind that scours the field
with fetch and haul of angry gusts
sweeps up a conflagration of
loose snow that whips and tears and strolls
across the acres lifting swirls
to twist and wobble like a ghost
of cyclone, DNA enlarged,
white dervish spinning into joy
and paradise of blinding cold
and deadly exaltation of
an angel wrestling turbulence.

SKIPPING

A carburetor skips, and rocks
will skip along the surface of
a pond. A fugitive will skip
the country if he can, and crooks
will skip the payment of their debts.
And one can walk content or run
with joy across a summer field.
But why omitting steps is such
a sign of pleasure's hard to say,
as if the gap and shift, the quick
eliding interruption of
a stride, reflects the shiver jolt,
releasing dance; accentuates,
as heart is said to skip a beat,
the lift, arrhythmic, breathless gasp
and rush and reach of crossing first
one threshold then another in
the vivid hop from foot to foot,
the hurrying toward and with delight.

IRONWEED

There is a shade of purple in
this flower near summer's end that makes
you proud to be alive in such
a world, and thrilled to know the gift
of sight. It seems a color sent
from memory or dream. In fields,
along old trails, at pasture edge,
the ironweed bares its vivid tint,
profoundest violet, a note
from farthest star and deepest time,
the glow of sacred royalty
and timbre of eternity
right here beside a dried-up stream.

A quick wet-weather spring appears
as plowing must be done in March,
a bleeding wound in garden soil.
But as the patch dries in the breeze,
the ground quits tickling out its spark
and merely glistens in the sun.
And when the crumbs of loose dirt bleach,
the bruise of dampness fades as rows
conceal the troubled source except
a faint depression that suggests
a hidden fracture under weeds
and summer drought, a secret voice
and vein now closed, like inspiration's
pulse, though buried deep and quiet,
awaiting summons by a storm.

BROWNFIELD

The lot that's poisoned by a spill
of toluene or gasoline
and tons of industrial swill
and drops of mercury dispersed
among the bits of asbestos
and rusting nails and tangled coils
with scattered beads of Styrofoam
all tossed among the posts and beams
of rotting wood and toads of grease,
exploded garbage bags and inks
on asphalt floes, and silty sinks,
is touched in one remote spot by
an ironweed's purple mystery.

LONE EAGLE

The countless flakes that shiver down
the trail between dark pines are thick
as history's greatest ticker-tape
parade on Broadway. Hear the roar
of crowds in boughs, applauding hands
in trees' remotest high recesses,
as wind swoops smoking, glittering snow
in honor of the hero of
the moment, in the long procession
of snowbird, mouse, and solo wren.

EXPULSION

When puddles dry in early June,
they leave a chalk line at the rims,
like drawings at a scene of crime
to mark the fall of victims.
The dust is bright as flowers that shed
their pollen on the breeze, which spread
on grass, can make our eyes swell red.
We step around the yellow hoops,
distorted topographic loops,
like lassos of the residue
flung out in fading effigies
of springtime's golden cruelties
that help us suffer Eden new.

HOMESICKNESS

Potatoes left in darkness keep
their eyes closed tightly, but
potatoes touched by hint of light
will sprout translucent shoots from eyes
that stretch and feel around and crawl
toward the illuminating source,
as though remembering a home
and luminous spark of vitality
in distant world and distant time,
across genetic memory
and evolution's tangled tree,
to germ of the original bloom
across the gulf of history.

JAR FLY

The cry is more a seethe than song,
high in the oaks, a call at once
bone-dry and juicy, blast so loud
it seems a thousand rattlesnakes
are giving furious warning,
so wild it's near impossible
to spot the source. The insect, called
cicada in most places, here
was known as jar fly, since the kids,
if they could catch one, sealed it in
a jar and watched its finger-small
anatomy vibrate inside
the amplifying bulb to light
the evening calm with serenade,
with fanfare, rasping anthem.
But what was usually found in woods
was not the tiny rock star itself
but just the husk of skin it shed
before it soared into the trees
to rock the lazy summer breeze
for hours on end with love ballad.

SKY GARDEN

Clouds smooth as odalisques lounge white
in eastern skies this afternoon,
the chisel-work of wind and height
on blinding vapor coiled, caressed
and polished by low Fahrenheit.
The hips and breasts go drifting to
the south, the cheeks luminous,
on the lofty, rare pavilion
of this gigantic harem.

The sound we hear from wind's other side
is not the trill of the hereafter.
No, the choral breeze arriving coincides
with sting of memory and things past,
with thrilling murmurs of crossed intent,
of traveling far and wandering in gusts
to find a listener. It is the dint
that stirs the grass and trees and clouds and sweeps
the dust away. It is the sweet lament
that stalks us from the country of the lost
and draws us back as to a mother
and won't be still and always finds an ear.

LINK

The cow that's cropping August grass
and swishing flies with deadly tail,
while blinking gnats from moist eyes,
is browsing toward the shadowy pines
like metal drawn to magnet's call.
She munches toward the noonday drowse
at the same speed as one high cloud.

NOVEMBER LIGHT

November light is like a dream,
no winter brightness yet, and fall's
extraordinary tints are all
receding, gray and brown, and seem
subdued as animals asleep
in dens and hollow trees and deep
in mud beneath the pond; the lint
of thistle, milkweed, goldenrod
lies white as frost and opalescent
on dying grass, at side of road.
A switch has been turned off: a lull
of outer space and inner world.
This light is like a spiritual
heard underground or from horizon,
Gregorian yet contemporary too,
a promise that some tasks are through.

TWO

PURPLE HANDS

If someone came to school with purple hands,
we knew they had been dropping taters. Spuds
cut up with eyes in every slice and wet
with starch and other chemicals had bled
on hands and stained the skin imperial.
We children tried to hide our mitts as though
ashamed to show—red-handed—we were made
to work. The purple not of royalty
or wealth but humble labor in the spring,
the ink of yet another hopeful planting,
when woods were luminous with dogwood blooms
and mists of red-tipped maples budding,
and towering otherworldly clouds looked down
on bets we placed in raw cold ground.

SQUIRT GUN

The orange see-through plastic makes
the gun at first appear red-hot.
The water in the grip is cool
and sloshes when you raise to aim.
The trigger slides the cylinder
and shoots a needle clear as light
across the porch to break as mist.
The gun is fun because it shoots
clear piss. You point and pee on leaves,
on ants, on flowers yards away.
You spray the sun and make rainbows
that melt away in instant rain.
You sprinkle dust along a step
and scare the cat again and hit
a june bug like a Messerschmitt.
And when the gun is almost dry,
you place the barrel between your lips
and close your eyes and fire a sip.

GO GENTLE

Was only when I watched my dad
approach his end I understood
how little Dylan Thomas knew
of death and dying. Any who
have sat beside a deathbed see
the most important thing at this
unique and most intense exit
is to accept and welcome that
good night. No greater horror could
be thought than witnessing a loved
one angry and in fear scream out
and hopelessly resist, deny
the step into the mystery,
and fight the certain fate of all.
That Dylan's powerful poem thrills
those far from any scene of death
can't be denied, and proves as truth
Plato's contention that verse lies,
and mostly feeds our vanities.
But those who keep the watch and stay
by one near passing on will pray
for calm and comforting assent
to the darkening firmament,
to the inevitable, as worth
far more than any rage or curse;
will plead for nothing but the right
and gentle passage to that night.

MILK SHAKE

First time I heard of such a thing,
I thought of milk stirred up to foam,
or beaten to a blue whipped cream.
And then at Asheville Dairy Bar,
my first trip to that lofty city,
I watched the jerk with paper cap
dump things into a blender, churn,
then pour the contents in a cup
to bring to me. A straw, stabbed through
the frothy top, drew up a sip—
and never had I savored such
ambrosia, so cold it stung
my taste buds and my tongue with grains
of ice and creamy essences;
and charged with flavor syrup on
the lips, the finest cold elixir
slurped in jubilation through
my teeth, across the mouth, and down
the throat with plenty more to come,
unfreezing just enough to swill
like mother's milk of happiness,
and sap of future opulence,
all gold and frankincense and myrrh
luxuriating mouth with thrill

of iced vanilla ichor, white
as julep of the angel host,
all mine for just two sweaty bits.

COUNTRY OF SUN

My neighbor who has cancer of the eye
goes walking on the road with careful lurch.
The mountainside is luminous with spring,
the blazing fogs of dogwood bloom and first
pink maple buds and tulip poplar flowers.
But he can only see the twilit air
of gray and shadows, pollen chalk outline
of dried-up puddles. Out he goes and then
returns and starts again, as slow as one
who feels his way in dark wind. Once
he stumbles but regains his stride and leans
with will into the blinding afternoon
as though trying to outwalk his pain,
or hoping to refind the country of sun.

AS ONE

I remember walking in a field,
so young the black-eyed Susans stared
me in the face, the air so bright
that every flick of grass was clear
and leaves seemed magnified. The flowers
stood tall and swayed—the daisies, Queen
Anne's lace, the Susans, yarrow—thrilled
the day and kept me company;
all level as a yard of water,
and made me feel as one of their
exploding, fierce community.

MANNA

In Sunday school they liked to tell
the story of the stuff that fell
in darkness for the Israelites
for forty years of desert nights.
I tried to visualize the drift
on dirt of this heavenly gift,
as cool and luminous and rich
as coconut or licorice,
for everyone to scoop and savor
on hands and knees, without labor,
the morsels clean as spring starlight,
and sweeter than a July night.
I dreamed and dreamed of such a feast
and woke again in tangled sheets.
But once I looked outside the room,
and saw new snow instead of gloom,
so white it seemed Elysium.

GREAT DAY IN THE MORNING

My father, when he was surprised
or suddenly impressed, would blurt
"Great day in the morning," as though
a revelation had struck him.
The figure of his speech would seem
to claim some large event appeared
at hand, if not already here;
a mighty day or luminous age
was flinging wide its doors as world
on world revealed their wonders in
the rapturous morning, always new,
beginning as the now took hold.

THE MARESLIDE

The long flat rock that drops so steep
down the mountainside above the creek
with winter ice locked on its face
seems some vast cameo encased
in darkened forests. Rumor says
a mare once reached the top and grazed
along the edge on autumn grass.
The rock was wet with slickest moss
and hooves slipped out as though on grease.
With screams the filly kicked in panic
and skidded down the mighty granite
and found no bench or ledge to slow
her plunge into the vale below,
which saw a horse shoot from the sky,
a thrashing, neighing meteorite.
But when I heard that sad story
and went to look while still a boy,
I wondered why no bones remained.
The story seemed as true as rain.

HOLE IN WATER

Whenever he heard something that
he found especially foolish, my
grandpa would laugh and say that's like
you stuck your finger in a pan
of water, took it out, and thought
a hole would still be there. He found
occasion to repeat the phrase
again, again, in his old age.

AUNT THARMUTHIAS

I had a great-aunt named Tharmuthias,
half sister of my grandpa Morgan (John).
We children never knew precisely how
her name was spelled or what it meant.
Her married name was Staton, and she lived
in Greenville, South Carolina, but we laughed
each time her name was spoken, told it was
a blessed given name from Scripture, though
none seemed to know exactly where the name
was found. I loved to hear the name and say
the name, Tharmuthias, like some strange call
from distant world and time and language hoard,
composed of precious metals, stones, with old
inscriptions, mystery box forever sealed.
It took me years to find Josephus had
recorded in his history of the Jews
that Pharaoh's daughter who they said would find
the infant Moses in bulrushes was
Thermuthis, princess of the royal blood.

BRINK

A couple walking with their child
in the deep river gorge hear first
a pop, and looking up around
the rim and cliffs above hear groans
and cracks machine gun–like and see
a giant oak begin to lean
and bark and fall with swish and swoosh
and sweep past brink and jut of wall
and stack of shale millennia thick
then down through towers of glittering air
and birds and shale and butterflies
and scent of stream to crash and bounce
and jolt the ground and break in tons
of rotten log and limbs and bark,
just where they stepped all unaware
in innocence, a nonce ago.

REACH

The kite we made from paper bags
and sourwood sprouts and masking tape
we carried to the pasture hill
and ran and let out string to loft
the flimsy shield into the wind.
It seemed a miracle: the sail
soared higher than the trees and then
above the ridge, would tug and veer
and dart and tremble like a trout,
then dive and settle till the air
returned. The mask of paper on
a cross of sticks would yield to weight
and sink but for the leash that made
it face the blast and rise. It was
the tension and restraint that let
it fly and play far out above
the next hedgerow, until, alas,
the zephyr stopped and no amount
of pull could reel it up or keep
the craft from limbs of tallest oak,
where it would lodge until next spring
to mark the reach of our elation.

THE YEARS AHEAD

When my grandpa took his produce
down the Winding Stairs to Greenville
to peddle door-to-door, he left
the day before and camped somewhere
near Travelers Rest just north of town.
After cooking by a campfire,
he slept beneath the wagon, since
the bed was heaped, and listened to
his horse crop grass and watched above
the trees the comet fling its ghost,
portending either ruin or
a century of wonder ahead.
Both interpretations were proclaimed.
Next morning he hitched up and drove
into the streets. He knew to go
to sections of the poor and of
the working middle class, for there
they paid the price he asked. The rich
and servants of the rich would haggle
and criticize his vegetables.
But ordinary people paid
more readily and more for beans
and squash, tomatoes, corn and hams.
He sold them frames of sourwood honey
and jugs of rich molasses made
the fall before. Only at the last

would he take the things unsold
to finer streets to dicker with
the servants of the quality.
And when the last jar of preserves
or jam was sold, he took the dimes
and quarters to the stores for cloth
and shoes, for cartridges and coffee,
sometimes a book, sometimes a doll.
And then he turned the wagon north
and rattled out the avenue
back toward the hills. And once he paid
a mesmerist who had a booth
beside the road to charm him, but
my grandpa's concentration was
so strong it broke the spell. And once
he paid a palmist to read his hand.
That night he camped beside the pike
but parked his wagon pointed south
to make a robber think he was
still loaded and not headed home
with cash that had to last throughout
another fall and winter. When
he looked up then and saw again
the comet's eerie plume that seemed
to write upon the sky, he thought
the portent good and years ahead

as golden as the leaves on hickories,
the future bright as the river,
or line that crossed his callused palm.

THREE

BACKWATER

I used to think backwater meant
remote or backward, out of date,
a place of stagnant poverty,
then found the term in history means
across the mountain watershed
where rivers run the other way
to west, to wilderness, to where
the future waits to open out
its shining promise, destiny.
Backwater meant new water then,
where greatness waited, tilted toward
the sunset rivers of hope where
the worst of us, the very worst
of all, might find a seventh chance.

APPLE HOWLING

Way back in Anglo-Saxon times,
the young men of the countryside
would gather New Year's Day in groves
of apple trees to shout a rhyme
and blast a horn and rap the trunks
with sticks, saluting dormant trees
in what was called a wassailing.
The tribute to the orchard begged
the trees to bring a richer yield,
a harvest weighing boughs of gold
down to the reach of children, bright
as jewels, the aromatic flesh
as cool and white as frost that turned
to foam on tooth and tongue, though now
the sugar slept in roots beneath
the snow and tracks of circling boys
who called the cidery sap in veins
to rise and rise and glimmer forth
as sun soared back behind the earth.

FRIENDLY FIRE

The legend is St. Francis begged
his aides to not put out the blaze
when once his robes caught fire. He said
be gentle to devouring flames,
respect the spirit of the bright
and hungry creature and the heat
that nourishes itself on cloth,
on wood. O Brother Fire, he cried,
be kind to me as I to you
and help me now to cauterize
my wound with your medicinal light
as I have nurtured you in need
and hunger, as our Savior does
sustain our breath through all our days—
and cooling time will quench our pain.

MEDICINE CIRCLES

White hunters on the plains
found rings of skulls of buffalo
and elk and sometimes skulls of wolves
and even human skulls, arranged
in careful circles on the grass,
in golgothas on level ground.
They understood the glaring hoops
were ceremonial sacred sites,
but asked what kind of medicine
was practiced in these halo walls.
Were circles pits for holy chants
or special invocations to
attract the mighty bison herds,
or yards for dances or for prayer?
Or were they merely signs to stars
and windy sky of presence and
ambition to make sense and form
of random residue of death,
or stage for comfort tokens of
mortality? White hunters at
the center of a ring felt power
and promise of their mission to
the wilderness and blessing for
their quest, but couldn't guess that in
a few decades they'd work a spell
themselves to fill horizon's ring
with death's-head bones that gleamed across

the emptiness, inspiring land
with burning wind and bitter dust
and white of different medicine,
in orbit round the blinding sun.

HORSE FIDDLE

To keep the squirrels from fields of corn,
and crows also, those farmers made
a kind of windmill out of rags
and rusty parts. Old wires and bits
of iron would scrape and scratch, screech out
like owls or ghosts when a faint breeze
would touch the rough contraption.
A scarecrow for the ears, the thing
they called a "horse fiddle" would cry
out loud and shriek like fiddlers mad,
or nails jerked on a blackboard. The rig
repelled the critters and the crows
like music in reverse. The air
was poisoned with cacophony.
But when the wind died down, the noise
would stop, and corn-attracted ones
slipped back from woods or flapped from pines
high on the ridge to savor milky
kernels and the music of stillness.

CONFEDERATE GRAVES AT ELMIRA

Of many hundred prisoners here
for little longer than a year,
about a fourth would never leave.
They died of plain starvation, grief;
of cholera, typhus, black frostbite.
To eat they caught a bird or rat
worth pennies or a worn-out blanket.
The local folks would pay a bit
to watch the johnnies from a tower.
Their medicine was sold and never
reached the reeking tents of suffering.
The flats along the wide Chemung
would flood and freeze and then, melting,
would freeze again. Each day more had
to be carried to the coffin shed
and carted to the field around
the hill. When April came the ground
thawed out to putrefaction.
Those who survived for celebration
of peace were loaded on the cars
and hauled back to the scenes of war's
calamity, the weaker dead
before they reached their charred homesteads.
It was a black custodian here
who dedicated twenty years
to finding out the name for each
Confederate grave and then had etched

the proper words on fields of stones,
to honor those lost far from home,
because it was the decent thing,
he answered neighbors' questioning.

NIGHT STAIRS

In cloisters of the Middle Ages,
the monks who said the offices
at two a.m. descended stairs
direct from dorm into the church
to say the night choir vigil, then
returned to sleep until matins
by stairs not seen except in dark.
The hidden steps led down to most
intensive chants in deepest night
and back to higher song of sleep
in lifelong practice of the rite
of hymn and sleep and steps between,
descent in dark to sing the paean,
ascent to sacrament of dream.

SHIELD

The Reverend Duffy Peyton Corn,
when answering a distant call
by mountain paths through hollows, thickets,
for his defense took only one
umbrella. If a panther, bear,
or mad dog leapt at him from brush,
he aimed the shaft at the attacker
and thrust the gadget open with
a whoosh. The wolf or other foe
would stop and back away, amazed
by sudden burst of tiny point
to giant mask with ribs and skin
as black as crow or bat. With shield
as light as cloth and quills, the Rev
would walk unharmed through miles and years
of wilderness, protected by
his nerve and fabric dark as ink,
and bright almost as shining words.

MONUMENTS

It's anybody's guess why folks
will keep old cars in yards and back
of houses: dead jalopies, trucks
and jeeps, a station wagon or
a van. They fade and peel and rust
with briars and honeysuckle vines
laced through the windows. Chromium
and headlights flash in noonday sun.
They're never sold for parts or scrap,
and trees grow through the fenders, shade
old hoods and trunks. Is there an urge
to save these heaps like memories?
Or is it loyalty to old friends,
the way a horse is put to grass
or loved dog kept when it's unfit?
Perhaps the presence of old chariots
and steeds gives continuity
to lives in veering change, the junk
like family monuments and signs
of sentimental worth, the house
surrounded by a host of spirits
and metal ghosts of days gone past,
with memories of speed and glamour,
preserved and honored, keeping watch
as ancestors are said to do,
or corpses consecrate a ground.

KUDZU COUSINS

What if the family tree was not
a tree but more a wilderness
of vines that curled and interlaced
across the hill of time far back
as we can see or comprehend?
The generations stagger back,
the marriages and cousins linked
in cross-connections knotted through
both shade and sunlight, drowning all
the other strains and names and blood
through tangles counter-woven
in this neck of the wilderness
where everyone is cousin once
or cousin twice or cousin once removed.

SINGING TO MAKE BUTTER COME

To coax the butter to appear, you raise
the plunger, drive it in the crock, and drive
it down again. But sometimes if it's hot
or if the air's too moist or pressure low,
no matter how you stir and dash and beat,
the clabber yields no butter. Sour milk stays
sour milk. You shake and beg the blinky swill,
and nothing makes the butter come. You feel
there's evil in the air, a curse is on
the chemistry and on your labor. Then's
the time to calm yourself and stay yourself
and whisper to the crock of clabber, sing
a slow, sad ballad or a hymn to soothe
the troubled sour. And soon the bits appear
like flakes of snow out of the depths, and more
rise like the dead at Resurrection, join
their tips and soaring bodies in the light
to form, from the corruption's thickening,
a sweet and firm and perfect gathering.

WALK ON WATER

Imagine gravity so charmed
the surface tension of the waves
won't tear, as if the laws of mass
had been reversed in some bright way,
so liquid depths could shoulder weight
that pressed on naked soles, or on
the soles of dusty sandals torn
from wandering desert sand as sharp
as broken glass. Imagine light
on water's tireless shivering
that made the human figure seem
to rise, to float, to journey forth
until a hand reached out to hand
and eye met eye and dry foot stepped
aboard the little craft adrift
above the suddenly thrashing deep.

CLOGGING

Now we gather in a circle,
turning right and turning leftward,
kicking as though threshing barley,
stomping as if crushing wine grapes,
clatter of our toe-taps ringing,
hammering down the seconds firmly,
trampling on the vines that trip us,
nailing note and nailing heartbeat,
stamping out the fires of petty,
stepping to the river's shiver,
cooling down the flames of anger,
summoning the ancient spirits
from the deepest wells and caverns,
from the secret mystery places,
beating back the blackest shadows,
raising dust of healing vapors
to the pulse of clap and laughter.

SINGING TO THE CORN

Sometimes farmers in a dry year,
instead of using hoe or plow,
which opened up the soil and let
the damp escape, would simply cut
or pull the weeds and sing to rows
of thirsty stalks. But corn loves rain,
loves rainy weather and wet soil,
prefers the riverbank and branch
and creek and edge of maple swamp.
Corn sends its roots down to the subsoil
to search for salts and minerals,
and sips and sucks the water table
to fuel its long, lush leaves and spurts
of jointed growth. But seasons when
the rain would never come, they found
that music helped to cool the field
in boiling noon and fatten seeds
on milky cobs as sweet as cream
or curds of sun, as if the song
drew moisture from the air like dew
to quench and flush the wilting leaves,
and pulled the grease from shining dirt
to plump the kernels tight as berries.
And singing soothed, inspired the hands
who labored on the baked, sharp clods
and sang for rain and harvest yield
and, joking, said the ears were thrilled.

IMMUNE

In far-back mountain coves they say
that walking barefoot in the snow,
the first snow of the season, will
prevent you catching cold all year.
Ten minutes stepping through the woods
will do the work, as though the shock
of bare soles on the ice will make
the flesh immune for months. Perhaps
the surge of energy to fight
the freezing wetness spurs resistance,
or maybe the humility
of going pilgrim-like into
the storm while others hide from frost
and bitter elements inspires
the blood to militance, to strength.
The naked soles in snow may be
like feet that step on beds of coals
in mystical ceremonies
to show that mind and nerves are free
above the pain's immensity.

LAND STEALER

The first surveyors on the western lands
across the mountains kept their compass hid,
for Indians *might* kill a hunter but
more likely take his furs and hides and rifle,
then let him go; but someone with a compass,
which Shawnees called "land stealer," was there
to measure earth and draw the land and mark
the boundaries of a claim to strip and settle.
The shiny instrument appeared a pool
in which the land thief looked to find the secrets
of future use and ownership. The needle
would quiver, flick its glittering tongue, and split
the land in pieces; scariest of all,
the tiny blade would tremble in a trance,
aligned with some far distant power unseen
beyond the clouds, beyond the north horizon,
remote as great white chief beyond the sea
who claimed the grass on which a thousand sires
had hunted, fought and danced and died, was his
by right divine, by mystery rite of royalty.
It was the heavy jewel in hand that held
the dart that brought the deadly medicine,
along with sicknesses innumerable.

SNAKES IN THE ATTIC

The attics of old houses prove
the perfect lairs for blacksnakes, sleek
blue racers, and ratcatchers too.
They climb through walls and air vents, live
in gloom and darkness just to feast
on mice and rats and birds up there,
so quiet that most of us don't know
we host them in the loft except
a swish above us late at night,
a rasp of scale and nail across
the ceiling when the house is still,
as yet another thief is snared
in ebony jaws and swallowed by
the resident but unseen spy.
The serpent in the space above's
no more a tempter than a dove,
and innocent as those below.

HOLY CUSSING

When the most intense revival swept
the mountains just a century ago,
participants described the shouts and barks
in unknown tongues, the jerks of those who tried
to climb the walls, the holy dance and laugh.
But strangest are reports of what was called
the holy cuss. Sometimes a man who spoke
in tongues and leapt for joy would break into
an avalanche of cursing that would stun
with brilliance and duration. Those that heard
would say the Holy Spirit spoke as from
a whirlwind. Words burned on the air like chains
of dynamite. The listeners were transfigured,
and felt true contact and true presence then,
as if the shock of unfamiliar
and blasphemous profanity broke through
beyond the reach of prayer and song and hollo
to answer heaven's anger with its echo.

OVERHEARD

The gate that swings in wind
in the high pasture seems
to have not only its
own rhythm but its own pace,
its own cadence and voice.
At times the gate groans, then
will shout as gusts surprise,
and fade to cricket stillness.
But in the milder breeze
the gate talks to itself,
mumbles strange phrases
as though meditating
(now lowing herds are gone)
which way it wants to sing
and what it wants to utter,
in mourning, or laughter.

The old timekeeper in its box,
an heirloom with a lisp and limp,
goes scratching out the seconds, dry,
as if time were an itch it had
to answer to. And then the tocks
sound like a drip or leak in time,
as though a giant reservoir
had cracked and seeped into the world
with no direction or intent,
except the skip of tiny drops
inexorably and downward sent
into the gulping vacuum.
And then the gulf is filled by chimes.

CRY NAKED

Those dying on a battlefield
or even in an accident
will tear away their clothes, it's said.
They'll rip aside their buttons, yank
at seams and buckles, peel away
the cloth and laces, even socks,
as though to die as naked as
the instant they were born, meet death
unhampered by possession or
disguise. Is it the urge to free
oneself of all restraint, confront
the mystery plain and without bond
or fashion, step bare-chested and
bare-assed into the dark from whence
we came, as poets claim to write
stripped bare and prophets cry out best
when naked in the wilderness?
As though our clothes might hide the self
that flowers and soars back out of time
as naked and as quick as light.

WATER OF DEATH

Those dying of a wound,
of massive bleeding, shock,
experience awful thirst,
as if they're parched by heat
of pain, as though they're drained
and bleached by suffering.
How human is the crave
for water's cooling splash
on tongue, in throat, the soothe
of chill and wetness down
into the belly, thrill
of sipping, thrill of swallow
and guzzle of communion,
the need to swill life's water
against time's ash and dust,
the drink of fellowship
to fill our veins, our guts,
with earth's most common element
just as we leave the earth.

SMELLS OF A CLOSET

At first you notice chemicals, the soaps,
detergents stored, and maybe kerosene,
and under those the scent of mothballs, mold,
old rubber of galoshes burned by age.
Behind the obvious smells rise fumes of wood
dried out for centuries, the resin cured
by many winters, stillness, locked in core
of amber of the heartwood honey. But
the farthest back of all, like smells from first
beginnings of the world, come whispering airs
that rose from crash and flash of the first fire
when darkness wept the stars and time began.

AWAKE

Old hunters in Kentucky said
the bears would not stir out of their
long hibernation till they heard
a blast of late spring thunder. When
the ground was shaken, air was rent,
the bruins woke and knew the weeds
were high enough to eat and grubs
along the creek were fat and sweet.
It was the crack of clashing skies
that roused them from their winter dreams
to feast on new luxuriance,
as shock of sudden cataclysm
will call us, like an orison.

REJECTS

There was a place near Kimble Branch
where chips of milk-white quartz spilled down
the bank like petals from a rock
that crumbled far above. These arrowheads
half-made and ruined, the slivers had
a cutting edge on each. We looked
for finished hunting points where some
old craftsman must have had his bench,
but found just fragments, bits of those
that cracked or shattered, and were flung,
rejected; no perfected ones.
The spoiled remained, but in the womb
of artistry the art was gone.

FLAG ON THE BARN

The old barn in the valley may
be weathered almost silver, but
a pole thrust from its ridge displays
the Stars and Stripes aflutter at
the tip. Such patriotic zeal
refreshes the lone traveler:
Old Glory, quickened by the wind
and shivery as a trout, stirs pulse,
stops breath, with streaming colors high
above the yard and cow stalls; pens
for chickens, hogs, and nursing calves;
above the heap of gold manure
that steams on winter mornings, smokes
a crown of flies at summer noon.
It thrills to think that loyalty
and dedication can extend
to hayloft, feed room, sty, and trough,
out this far in a distant cove.
As wind shifts suddenly, the limbs
of poplars pledge allegiance.
And when the wind goes still, the flag
hangs brighter than a bloodstained rag.

HILLSIDE PLOW

The hillside plow's a Janus tool.
The blade can turn to left or right
for cultivating steepest slopes,
and dirt is always thrown downhill;
the moldboard rips the furrows right,
then, flipping the blade over, you
return by curling soil to left,
and row by row and year by year,
you throw the topsoil down the ridge
to answer pull of washing rain,
to answer slurp of gravity,
by means of this one instrument,
adaptable and oiled and sharp,
on acres steep as a church roof,
on acres you could fall out of.

MOUND BUILDERS

The Creeks of frontier Georgia said
they made the mounds along the streams
for sanctuaries during floods.
When rivers spread across the plain,
they climbed atop the fashioned hills
until the inundation passed.
But later studies would reveal
the elevations packed with bones
and grave goods: spears and arrowheads,
ceramics, gems, totemic signs,
and favorite beads. It seems the Creeks
deposited their dead, their kin,
in ceremonial heaps that took
a dozen generations to
attain the height desired. They may
have sought a refuge from the floods
on those acclivities, but what
they stood atop and slept atop
for safety was the sacred dirt
and relics of their clan, the signs
and symbols of their hearth, beliefs
and arts and holy bundles too,
as all of us rely, and must,
on our traditions and the deep
ancestral memories and ways
to bear us up and get us through
the deadly and uncertain days,

sustaining breath and sight and hope
on residue and legacy
of those beloved who came before
and watch us from the glittering stars.

Robert Morgan is the author of *Boone*, a biography
of Daniel Boone, and the bestselling novel *Gap Creek*,
among numerous other novels and story collections.
He has written twelve books of poems and is the
recipient of many honors, including the James G.
Hanes Poetry Prize from the Fellowship of Southern
Writers and an Academy Award from the American
Academy of Arts and Letters. He lives in Ithaca,
New York.

JOHN ASHBERY
Selected Poems
Self-Portrait in a Convex Mirror

TED BERRIGAN
The Sonnets

LAUREN BERRY
The Lifting Dress

JOE BONOMO
Installations

PHILIP BOOTH
Selves

JIM CARROLL
Fear of Dreaming: The
*   Selected Poems*
Living at the Movies
Void of Course

ALISON HAWTHORNE DEMING
Genius Loci
Rope

CARL DENNIS
Callings
New and Selected Poems
*   1974–2004*
Practical Gods
Ranking the Wishes
Unknown Friends

DIANE DI PRIMA
Loba

STUART DISCHELL
Backwards Days
Dig Safe

STEPHEN DOBYNS
Velocities: New and Selected
*   Poems, 1966–1992*

EDWARD DORN
Way More West: New and
*   Selected Poems*

ADAM FOULDS
The Broken Word

CARRIE FOUNTAIN
Burn Lake

AMY GERSTLER
Crown of Weeds: Poems
Dearest Creature
Ghost Girl
Medicine
Nerve Storm

EUGENE GLORIA
Drivers at the Short-Time Motel
Hoodlum Birds

DEBORA GREGER
Desert Fathers, Uranium
*   Daughters*
God
Men, Women, and Ghosts
Western Art

TERRANCE HAYES
Hip Logic
Lighthead
Wind in a Box

ROBERT HUNTER
Sentinel and Other Poems

MARY KARR
Viper Rum

WILLIAM KECKLER
Sanskrit of the Body

JACK KEROUAC
Book of Sketches
Book of Blues
Book of Haikus

JOANNA KLINK
Circadian
Raptus

JOANNE KYGER
As Ever: Selected Poems

ANN LAUTERBACH
Hum
If in Time: Selected Poems,
*   1975–2000*
On a Stair
Or to Begin Again

CORINNE LEE
PYX

PHILLIS LEVIN
May Day
Mercury

WILLIAM LOGAN
Macbeth in Venice
Strange Flesh
The Whispering Gallery

ADRIAN MATEJKA
Mixology

MICHAEL MCCLURE
Huge Dreams: San Francisco
*   and Beat Poems*

DAVID MELTZER
David's Copy: The Selected
*   Poems of David Meltzer*

ROBERT MORGAN
Terroir

CAROL MUSKE-DUKES
An Octave Above Thunder
Red Trousseau
Twin Cities

ALICE NOTLEY
Culture of One
The Descent of Alette
Disobedience
In the Pines
Mysteries of Small Houses

LAWRENCE RAAB
The History of Forgetting
Visible Signs: New and
*   Selected Poems*

BARBARA RAS
The Last Skin
One Hidden Stuff

PATTIANN ROGERS
Generations
Wayfare

WILLIAM STOBB
Absentia
Nervous Systems

TRYFON TOLIDES
An Almost Pure Empty
*   Walking*

ANNE WALDMAN
Kill or Cure
Manatee/Humanity
Structure of the World
*   Compared to a Bubble*

JAMES WELCH
Riding the Earthboy 40

PHILIP WHALEN
Overtime: Selected Poems

ROBERT WRIGLEY
Beautiful Country
Earthly Meditations: New and
*   Selected Poems*
Lives of the Animals
Reign of Snakes

MARK YAKICH
The Importance of Peeling
*   Potatoes in Ukraine*
Unrelated Individuals Forming
*   a Group Waiting to Cross*

JOHN YAU
Borrowed Love Poems
Paradiso Diaspora

Printed in the United States
by Baker & Taylor Publisher Services